Lil Legends

First learning book of vegetables

pumpkin

carrot

green peas

broccoli

cauliflower

eggplants

cucumber

french beans

asparagus

spinach

cabbage

bell pepper

beetroot

turnip

potato

tomato

lettuce

onion

sweet potato

okra

pumpkin

carrot

green peas

broccoli

cauliflower

eggplants

cucumber

french beans

asparagus

spinach

cabbage

bell pepper

beetroot

turnip

potato

tomato

lettuce

onion

sweet potato

okra